PRAYER

ANDRÉ GORHAM

PRAYER

Copyright © 2008 by André Gorham

ISBN: 978-0-9786581-6-8

Published by

LIFEBRIDGE

BOOKS

P.O. BOX 49428
CHARLOTTE, NC 28277

Printed in the United States of America.

DEDICATION

*This book is dedicated to the people of
Southeast Asia who were born again, healed,
delivered, blessed and encouraged as a direct result
of believing prayers to Almighty God.*

"André Gorham's teaching on prayer is a boon to the body of Christ. Believers, who will practice what he teaches about prayer, can expect miracles and answered prayers on a regular basis."
REV. ARSENIO G. BONIFACIO II, HOME OF THE LORD CHRISTIAN ASSEMBLY, MANDALUYONG CITY, PHILIPPINES

"Want a quantum leap in your relationship with God and in overcoming the battles in your life? Then read this book. It will draw you into an intimacy with our Heavenly Father that will pleasantly surprise and thrill you."
ATTORNEY ELWOOD BECTON, RALEIGH, NC

"Pastor André's teachings on prayer come deeply from his personal life and are filled with meaningful insight."
THE HONORABLE GEORGE S. SCHULZE PHILIPPINO CONSUL A. H. OF THE REPUBLIC OF HAITI. ALABANG, PHILIPPINES

"I endorse this book as a 'must have' resource for pastors, leaders and anyone interested in improving their prayer life."
JAMES D. SMITH, B.S., C.P.M., NATIONAL DIRECTOR, FULL GOSPEL BUSINESSMEN'S FELLOWSHIP INTERNATIONAL, RALEIGH, NC

"Pastor Gorham calls the church to the highest spiritual discipline of prayer as one who himself has entered into the Holy of Holies through prayer."
REV. MICHAEL R. SMITH, SR., CROSS OF CHRIST DISCIPLESHIP MINISTRIES, WAKE FOREST, NC

"This book is not only an excellent study on prayer, but to us a reflection of the life of a man of prayer we've known for over 20 years."
REV. JIM URBAN, MISSIONARY TO THE PHILIPPINES, BRANSON, MO

CONTENTS

INTRODUCTION

I f you purchase a brand new computer with the latest software, it will take time to learn how these innovative programs operate. It's the same with a new relationship. You begin asking yourself, "What do I need to know about this person to make our friendship work?"

As a new Christian, one of the first things we are told is, "Read your Bible and pray." We know how to read, but what about prayer? It is an activity we are supposed to automatically understand.

As you will discover on these pages, God has instituted prayer as a means for you to have personal fellowship and communion with Him, but there is much we need to learn. For example:

- Exactly how does prayer work?
- Why do we need to be specific when we pray?
- What does the Bible say regarding how long we should pray?
- What are the "weapons of our warfare"?
- Why did Jesus pray while He was on earth?
- Can I be certain God is listening?

- What personal characteristics do I need to possess to be successful in prayer?
- What preparations do I need to make before calling on the Lord?
- What is involved in a prayer of agreement?
- How can I form an eternal partnership with God?

These are just a few of the questions we will answer in this book.

The final section, "10 Checkpoints" is written for you to evaluate your spiritual progress. You will find Scripture references you can use in your personal devotions or for discussion starters for small group study. In addition, I have included "A Personal Prayer and Bible Reading Plan" which will help your spiritual growth.

I trust you are ready to experience a deeper relationship with the Lord and see Him answer the desires of your heart through the awesome power of prayer.

– André Gorham

CHAPTER 1

HOW AND WHY PRAYER WORKS

It is only human nature to question what we don't understand. This is why we ask: Do we truly hear from Heaven? Will God move on my behalf? Exactly how does prayer work? And why does it work?

You are not the first person on this planet who has bombarded Heaven with your prayers—and you will not be the last. There have been untold millions of Christians since Christ died on the cross and was raised from the dead who have called on His name and received answers.

SIX REASONS PRAYER WORKS

My purpose in writing this book is to help you grasp the power and significance of your fellowship and communion with Almighty God. As we begin, let me share six reasons why this beautiful, glorious gift called prayer is alive and working today in the lives of believers.

1. Prayer works because the Father loves us.

What does God think of us, His children? While He loves everyone in the world—believer and non-believer alike—He shares a special bond with those who are in the household of faith. Remember, *"At that day ye shall ask in my name: and I say not unto you, that I will pray the Father for you: For the Father himself loveth you, because ye have loved me, and have believed that I came out from God"* (John 16:26-27).

The reason the Father instituted
this system of communication is so
we can spend quality time and develop a
deep and intimate fellowship with Him.

As a result of this loving relationship, God hears and answers our prayers. Scripture declares, *"Because he hath set his love upon me, therefore will I deliver him: I will set him on high, because he hath known my name. He shall call upon me, and I will answer him: I will be with him in trouble; I will deliver him, and honour him"* (Psalm 91:14-15).

These words of the psalmist make it clear that help from above is the direct result of loving God, and calling on His holy name.

The reason the Lord cares so much for you is because you are part of His family—His child. *"Behold, what manner of love the Father hath bestowed upon us, that we should be called the sons of God"* (1 John 3:1). Then we are told, *"Beloved, now are we the sons of God..."* (v.2).

For many, the reference point for prayer is a crisis or some personal desire. But the reason supplication is effective is not based on our need, rather it is because our Heavenly Father loves us.

2. Prayer works because of the infrastructure established by the work of Christ at Calvary.

In God's sight, answered prayers are a legal act. This is because of the death, burial and resurrection of Jesus. The "infrastructure" or divine system for approaching the Father is now in place.

We can access God in Jesus' name. Scripture promises, *"This is the covenant that I will make with them after those days, saith the Lord, I will put my laws into their hearts, and in their minds will I write them; and their sins and iniquities will I remember no more"* (Hebrews 10:16-17).

This gives us *"...boldness to enter into the holiest by the blood of Jesus, by a new and living way, which he hath consecrated for us, through the veil, that is to say, his flesh"* (vv.19-20).

How exciting! You have full, unlimited access to the Father. Jesus did away with the sin nature—removing the barrier which separated you from God.

Since there is no longer a partition between us, we can act upon His Word which says, *"Let us therefore come boldly unto the throne of grace, that we may obtain mercy, and find grace to help in time of need"* (Hebrews 4:16).

We now have confidence to commune with the Father in prayer because Christ established the arrangement legally. As a result, I can talk to God in the name of Jesus and expect results.

Yes, He shed His blood on the cross when the crown of thorns was pushed into His head and His body was pierced with a spear by a Roman soldier. But it is the precious blood which was offered by God's Son in Heaven's Holy of Holies which gives us free access to the Father.

At the Last Supper, Jesus told His disciples, *"This cup is the new testament in my blood, which is shed for you"* (Luke 22:20). He ratified, or set in motion, His work through His blood—providing a basis for answered prayer.

From the birth of Christ to His completed work, there was an ordained plan. When you call on the Lord, He will hear you—and do more than you can ask or think.

When Mary, a virgin, was chosen by the Father to bear a child, the angel appeared to her, saying, *"For with God, nothing shall be impossible"* (Luke 1:37).

Today, nothing has changed. Because of the work of Christ, you can expect your petitions to be answered.

3. Prayer works because we are God's elect.

The Lord has not only chosen you, He has *recreated* you from the inside out. As the Bible assures us, *"Therefore if any man be in Christ, he is a new creature: old things are passed away; behold, all things*

13

are become new" (2 Corinthians 5:17).

From this moment forward, you are one of God's elect—selected by the Father and adopted into His family.

In the book of James we are told, *"Is any among you afflicted? let him pray. Is any merry? let him sing psalms. Is any sick among you? let him call for the elders of the church; and let them pray over him, anointing him with oil in the name of the Lord: and the prayer of faith shall save the sick, and the Lord shall raise him up; and if he have committed sins, they shall be forgiven him"* (James 5:13-15).

All this is possible for the elect of God. In His sight you are *"...as lively stones...an holy priesthood, to offer up spiritual sacrifices, acceptable to God by Jesus Christ"* (1 Peter 2:5). Even more, the Bible says, *"...ye are a chosen generation, a royal priesthood, an holy nation, a peculiar people; that ye should show forth the praises of him who hath called you out of darkness into his marvellous light: which in time past were not a people, but are now the people of God..."* (vv.9-10).

If we truly are "God's people," no request is too big for Him to answer.

The Lord proclaims, *"If my people, which are called by my name, shall humble themselves, and pray, and seek my face, and turn from their wicked ways; then will I hear from heaven, and will forgive their sin, and will heal their land"* (2 Chronicles 7:14).

As the *"elect of God"* (Colossians 3:12), you have the right to seek His face and receive the blessings of heaven.

4. Prayer works because we are the righteousness of God in Christ Jesus.

I trust you fully appreciate what transpires when you give your heart to the Lord. Suddenly you have a new position in the Kingdom. As the Bible tells us, *"For he hath made him to be sin for us, who knew no sin; that we might be made the righteousness of God in him"* (2 Corinthians 5:21).

There is nothing you could ever do to earn this status. It cannot be bestowed by an organization, a church or a denomination. Christ provided for your righteousness on the cross and we receive it in Jesus' name. Because we have accepted salvation by faith, *"...we are ambassadors for Christ"* (v.20).

Since we are righteous, we can speak one-on-One to the Lord and receive answers. *"For the eyes of the*

Lord are over the righteous, and his ears are open unto their prayers..." (1 Peter 3:12).

In James 5:16 we find these prayer-answering words: "Confess your faults one to another, and pray one for another, that ye may be healed. The effectual fervent prayer of a righteous man availeth much."

This is why prayer works!

You can approach the Father and believe for whatever you desire according to Mark 11:24 —and see miraculous results.

As a pastor and a believer, I have listened to Christians literally beg God to answer some particular urgent need—thinking it's the only time the Lord is going to listen to them.

This attitude is not based on biblical principles. It is very much like assuming your washer and dryer are only going to function when your clothes are the dirtiest. No, these devices were designed to operate *all* the time!

So it is with prayer, which does not wait for an emergency, but works continually—24/7, 365 days a year.

Whether you *avail* yourself of this privilege is another matter altogether.

—————— ❥ ——————

*Regardless of our attitude or
thinking, prayer works!*

This is why we are told to approach the Father for *everything*. The apostle Paul explains it this way: *"Be careful for nothing; but in every thing by prayer and supplication with thanksgiving let your requests be made known unto God"* (Philippians 4:6).

What will be the result? The *"...peace of God, which passeth all understanding, shall keep your hearts and minds through Christ Jesus"* (v.7).

As the "righteous of God" we have this divine pledge: *"He that spared not his own Son, but delivered him up for us all, how shall he not with him also freely give us all things?"* (Romans 8:32).

To paraphrase, how is it possible—physically, intellectually, emotionally, mentally, psychologically, spiritually, or in any way—that God would give Jesus Christ to us without also freely making everything in His Kingdom available?

Then we read this rhetorical question: *"Who shall separate us from the love of Christ? shall tribulation, or distress, or persecution, or famine, or nakedness, or peril, or sword?"*(v.35).

The answer is a resounding "No!" Because *"...in all these things we are more than conquerors through him that loved us"* (v.37).

We are righteous—not in the sweet bye and bye, but in the here and now! As a result, God is listening, and answers us when we call on Him.

5. Prayer works because we have His Word and His will.

The more you delve into Scripture, the more you find that the will of God is found in His Word. *"And this is the confidence that we have in him, that, if we ask any thing according to his will, he heareth us. And if we know that he hear us, whatsoever we ask, we know that we have the petitions that we desired of him"* (1 John 5:14-15).

How can you be assured God hears you? By meeting the Lord's conditions, it is guaranteed—but there is an "if" involved. According to Scripture, *"If ye abide in me, and my words abide in you, ye shall ask what ye will, and it shall be done unto you"*(John 15:7).

Notice, the Lord says you can ask what you will and it shall be done. This is possible because once you hold the Word in your heart and soul, you know what

God wants—so your requests will be in accordance with *His* will.

By studying Scripture you can say with assurance, "This is what the Lord desires for me." Among other blessings, He wants you to enjoy health, abundance and peace. The Bible shares this in great detail.

Give yourself to the Word—not being swayed by your emotions or feelings.

Don't be distracted by what others say, just open the pages of the Bible to learn how to function and succeed according to God's will.

This empowers you to take action on divine principles. As James counsels, *"But be ye doers of the word, and not hearers only, deceiving your own selves. For if any be a hearer of the word, and not a doer, he is like unto a man beholding his natural face in a glass: For he beholdeth himself, and goeth his way, and straightway forgetteth what manner of man he was. But whoso looketh into the perfect law of liberty, and continueth therein, he being not a forgetful hearer, but a doer of the work, this man shall be blessed in his deed"* (James 1:22-25).

If you have accepted Christ as your Savior, you

have the power to *do* the Word and the will of God. Remember, you have been set apart, or sanctified by the Father (Hebrews 10:14).

When you pray, you can know what the Lord has planned. Why? Because, *"...we have the mind of Christ"* (1 Corinthians 2:16).

Are you armed with the Word of God? If so you will pray according to His will—which is the key to seeing results.

6. Prayer works because we can have what we desire when we pray specifically.

Total belief for a particular answer is at the heart of successful prayer. Jesus gives us this amazing promise: *"For verily I say unto you, That whosoever shall say unto this mountain, Be thou removed, and be thou cast into the sea; and shall not doubt in his heart, but shall believe that those things which he saith shall come to pass; he shall have whatsoever he saith. Therefore I say unto you, What things soever ye desire, when ye pray, believe that ye receive them, and ye shall have them"* (Mark 11:23-24).

Instead of petitioning in general terms, be specific. Many are far too vague or obscure in their prayer time, saying, "Lord, whatever you want to do will be just fine." But God wants you to be precise when you ask.

In the city of Jericho, a blind beggar named Bartimaeus heard that Jesus was passing by and called out to Him, *"...have mercy on me"* (Mark 10:47).

Of course the Lord knew he was blind, but wanted to hear his specific request. So He asked him, *"What wilt thou that I should do unto thee?"* (v.51).

Bartimaeus replied, *"Lord, that I might receive my sight"*

At that moment he was instantly healed.

Yes, God knows your need, but He longs for you to tell Him.

HE WILL ANSWER

For more than two decades of my adult life I have enjoyed the fruits of answered prayer. From personal experience I can assure you, *"... he will be very gracious unto thee at the voice of thy cry; when he shall hear it, he will answer thee"* (Isaiah 30:19).

Praise God. Prayer works!

CHAPTER 2

FIVE KEYS TO EFFECTUAL PRAYER

S adly, there are those who conclude prayer is nothing more than an exercise in futility. One person even told me, "I think answered prayer is just mere coincidence."

Far from it. Millions can testify to how God has intervened on their behalf.

One of the foundational verses on this topic is: *"The effectual fervent prayer of a righteous man availeth much"* (James 5:16).

The word "effectual" has two meanings: (1) to *achieve* the desired results and (2) to *produce* the desired results.

I like both definitions because if you are going to pray you expect answers. James gives this example of what happens when a righteous person calls on God:

"*Elias* [Elijah] *was a man subject to like passions as we are, and he prayed earnestly that it might not rain: and it rained not on the earth by the space of three years and six months. And he prayed again, and the heaven gave rain, and the earth brought forth her fruit*" (vv.17-18).

———— 🪶 ————

We don't pray for things to remain status quo, rather to invite God to enter the scene and produce a positive transformation.

Most important, don't simply call on Him because you desire a certain result. First, seek God's face until you are sure in your heart God will do it for you (1 John 3:19-22).

In my own experience, when I realized the Lord was more than willing to pour out His blessings upon me, my prayer life became joy unspeakable. As Jesus tells us, *"Fear not, little flock; for it is your Father's good pleasure to give you the kingdom"* (Luke 12:32).

We are counseled, *"... men ought always to pray, and not to faint"* (Luke 18:1).

Why would you continue petitioning God if He turns a deaf ear? But when the Lord opens the floodgates of heaven it give us fuel to keep on praying.

THE FIVE KEYS

Let me share five proven keys to effectual prayer. These are simple, yet extremely significant:

1. Before you pray, you must believe.

Our belief must precede our prayer—not as an afterthought. You may admit, "Well, I'm not yet at that point in my spiritual life."

Then make a concerted effort to study the Word, read solid material on building your faith—including my own book, *Faith Works*—and listen to anointed messages on the topic. Do whatever it takes to bolster and strengthen your belief system.

According to Scripture, *"...without faith, it is impossible to please Him: for he that cometh to God must believe that He is, and that He is a rewarder of them that diligently seek Him"* (Hebrews 11:6).

Before you even approach God, you have to first believe. For example, let's say you are praying for circumstances to change in your finances or perhaps heal a broken relationship with a family member. Ask yourself, "What do I presently believe about this problem?"

25

If what you believe does not coincide with your prayer, it's time to change your believing!

- It is a contradiction to approach God believing in sickness yet wanting healing.
- It is a contradiction to approach God believing in divorce yet wanting a healthy marriage.
- It is a contradiction to approach God believing in poverty and lack then asking for His abundance.

There must be agreement. You have to divest yourself of the unbelief associated with what you are praying for.

Will you receive everything you ask God for? Probably not. It's only *"...what ye shall ask in prayer, believing, ye shall receive"* (Matthew 21:22). The key words are "in prayer" and "believing."

Next, when you act upon your belief you are exercising faith. This is what took place when two sightless men cried out for Jesus to heal them. The Lord asked, *"Believe ye that I am able to do this?"* (Matthew 9:28).

They answered, *"Yea, Lord"* (v.28).

Jesus touched their eyes and said, *"According to*

your faith be it unto you" (v.29).

Their sight returned at that very moment—because they acted on their belief and sought out Jesus.

The hinge on which the door of effectual prayer swings open is your believing. And when you step out in faith, miracles abound.

You see, prayer is the posture of confidence, assurance, boldness and full persuasion that God will work on your behalf.

Are you asking, knocking, seeking and finding? Remember, *"...faith without works is dead"* (James 2:20).

Calling on God with total belief produces a manifestation. You will then see the results. God says, *"Ask of me, and I will give thee the heathen for your inheritance, and the uttermost parts of the earth for your possession"* (Psalm 2:8).

Are you ready to see answers? Develop your believing!

2. Know the Word.

Your prayer life will be much more effective when you know what the Bible has to say concerning the things for which you are calling on God. Otherwise, you are searching in the dark—just hoping and groping.

Your true answers for life will not be found in human research or logic. Keep asking yourself, "What does the Word say?"

- In good times and bad, what does the Word say?
- When the economy is booming or when it goes bust, what does the Word say?
- When the skies are clear or a storm is brewing, what does the Word say?

Everyone needs a barometer more reliable than feelings or emotions! Knowing God's principles will give you confidence in every situation.

When you hide the Word in your heart and *"...walk in the light, as he is in the light..."* (1 John 1:7), your fellowship with the Father thrives—and your prayers will be based on what you have learned from Scripture.

As I open the pages of the Bible, I see the *"perfect law of liberty"* (James 1:25) which gives me guidance and direction on how I am to pray. It shows the will of

God in action—for *me!*

The only prayers God will not answer are those which are not uttered according to His will. This is why we must seek His face, hear His voice and follow the leading of the Holy Spirit.

We should be *"Praying always with all prayer and supplication in the Spirit"* (Ephesians 6:18).

Where do we learn how to pray effectively?
By studying the Word.

3. Cast your cares upon the Lord.

If you are weary of going it alone and are ready to enter into a holy alliance and spiritual allegiance with God, make the decision to release whatever weighs you down and let the Lord take care of you as He has promised.

Here's the path to take: *"Humble yourselves therefore under the mighty hand of God, that he may exalt you in due time: Casting all your care upon him; for he careth for you"* (1 Peter 5:6-7).

Why carry the burden one day longer? Remember, *"...the cares of this world, and the deceitfulness of riches, and the lusts of other things entering in, choke the word, and it becometh unfruitful"* (Mark 4:19).

No mater how great the problem, hand it over to God and say, "Father, I know you love me and I can't deal with this difficulty anymore. In the name of Jesus, I am giving this to You. Thank You for lifting the weight from my shoulders."

———— ✌ ————

Don't worry if the manifestation isn't evident instantly. When you do your part, the Lord will do His.

Once you have released the burden to God, don't remain anxious or have second thoughts. The apostle Paul admonishes, *"Be careful for nothing; but in every thing by prayer and supplication with thanksgiving let your requests be made known unto God"* (Philippians 4:6).

Instead of agonizing over your financial situation alone, or worrying about a broken relationship, allow God to become your partner.

Let go and let God!

4. Pray with thanksgiving.

In giving thanks to the Lord you are basically

saying, "I know God has heard me, so as an expression of my faith and as an act of my believing, I am thanking Him."

Your gratitude should be all-encompassing. The Bible tells us, *"In everything, give thanks: for this is the will of God in Christ Jesus concerning you"* (1 Thessalonians 5:18).

Regardless of what is taking place in your life, be grateful your Heavenly Father is greater than anything you are facing.

God doesn't promise He will take you out of the problem, but <u>through</u> it (Isaiah 43:1-5).

As the psalmist writes, *"Yea, though I walk through the valley of the shadow of death, I will fear no evil: for thou art with me; thy rod and thy staff they comfort me"* (Psalm 23:4).

Our thanksgiving is an act of faith and an expression of belief. It is God's desire that *"...men pray everywhere, lifting up holy hands, without wrath and doubting"* (1 Timothy 2:8). At every opportunity demonstrate how thankful you truly are—sing, shout, perhaps do a little dance. You can rejoice and celebrate because the Father has heard your prayer.

If the Son of God thanked His Father, how can we do anything less?

In a place called Bethany, Jesus went to the tomb of Lazarus, who had been dead for four days. There, he ordered that the stone be removed from the front of the cave which contained the man's body.

Scripture records how *"...Jesus lifted up his eyes, and said, Father, I thank thee that thou hast heard me. And I knew that thou hearest me always: but because of the people which stand by I said it, that they may believe that thou hast sent me. And when he thus had spoken, he cried with a loud voice, Lazarus, come forth"* (John 11:41-43).

Thanksgiving preceded a mighty miracle.

Personally, I thank God for what He has done in my past, what He is doing today, and for what He will do in my future. This "attitude of gratitude" is not only something I heard on a tape or read in a book, it is my life style.

The most effective way to begin your prayer time is with a heart overflowing with appreciation: *"Let us come before his presence with thanksgiving... "*(Psalms 95:2). And your gratitude should never end: *"Continue in prayer, and watch...with thanksgiving"* (Colossians 4:2).

5. Don't stop praying until the answer arrives.

We are told to *"Pray without ceasing"* (1 Thessalonians 5:17). In simple language, don't quit!

Stay before the Lord until the result occurs. Impatiently, you may ask, "Well, how long does it take?" Until you receive the answer.

Many become "drop outs" on their way to receiving from God. Here are just a few of their reasons:

- They doubt God really hears them.
- They don't think they are worthy.
- They have unconfessed sin.
- They become distracted by the pressures of life.
- They listen to the lies of Satan.

Friend, remain strong and resist yielding to the *temptation* to stop praying.

Sure, there are times when doubt causes us to

derail, but with God's help we can take the necessary steps to get back on track. Look at your heart, listen to your words and examine your thoughts. Are they building faith and expectation?

To counter unbelief, approach the Lord with total trust, stand on the Word, give Him your burden and begin to praise and thank Him.

It is God's desire for you to be healthy. *"Beloved, I wish above all things that thou mayest prosper and be in health, even as thy soul prospereth"* 3 John 2).

The question is, what do *you* want?

You may answer, "I want to be healed." Are you being honest? Then why do your words suggest God may not want you to be well:

- "He is trying to teach me something."
- "It's a genetic problem in our family."
- "It may not be His will."

Why talk yourself out of what the Father desires? Through prayer you can bring heaven into your situation.

The Almighty is not looking down from above, saying, "Well, they have suffered long enough, I think I will bless them."

No, that's not how the Father operates. To find out what is causing a short-circuit in your prayer life, take an introspective look. It may be nothing more than the fact you just don't believe God will answer this particular need. Take time with the Lord to rebuild your faith.

Remember, we are *"...always to pray and not to faint"* (Luke 18:1).

Keep praying!

CHAPTER 3

PRAYER POWER

In the early days of the church, when the ministry of the apostles was rapidly multiplying and thousands were coming to Christ, problems arose which needed to be urgently addressed.

In Acts 6 we learn how hard feelings developed among the Greek-speaking believers who thought their widows were being discriminated against in the daily food distribution.

So *"...the twelve called the multitude of the disciples unto them, and said, It is not reason that we should leave the word of God, and serve tables"* (Acts 6:2).

These anointed men knew their calling and prioritized their walk with God. Their mission was clear: the Word of God and prayer must be their primary responsibilities.

Spiritual Priorities

Being influenced by the flesh, or your senses, will never give you the victory you are looking for.

How did the apostles resolve the problem they faced with the Greek believers? It was by making a commitment to the power of prayer. They reasoned, *"Wherefore, brethren, look ye out among you seven men of honest report, full of the Holy Ghost and wisdom, whom we may appoint over this business. But we will give ourselves continually to prayer, and to the ministry of the word"* (Acts 6:3-4).

They were saying, "Listen, there is a group of people who should shoulder this responsibility, but as your leaders, we don't feel we should abandon our calling to function in an administrative capacity, taking care of the widows. We are asking you to handle this physical problem and we will give ourselves totally to prayer and to the spiritual ministry of God's Word."

This was a quality decision and the congregation was pleased with the idea. They chose, *"...Stephen, a man full of faith and of the Holy Ghost, and Philip, and Prochorus, and Nicanor, and Timon, and Parmenas, and Nicolas a proselyte of Antioch: Whom they set before the apostles: and when they had prayed, they laid their hands on them"* (vv.5-6).

What was the result? Scripture chronicles: *"...the word of God increased; and the number of the disciples multiplied in Jerusalem greatly; and a great company of the priests were obedient to the faith"* (v.7).

Prioritizing prayer allowed the apostles to expand the Kingdom.

AN UNDERAPPRECIATED RESOURCE

I am convinced it is in the best interest of every pastor, church, denomination and believer to make the same wise choice. If you long to see God's power at work, realize it comes only through prayer.

There are blessings we will miss and objectives which will never be reached unless we are in constant communication with our Heavenly Father.

Sadly, for many Christian, prayer is their most underappreciated resource. I regularly meet people who have gone days, weeks, even months without personally calling on God. Since our Heavenly Father has given us this unlimited and dynamic access, we are only short-changing ourselves if we don't exercise this gift.

Have you made prayer a daily habit?

The apostles did—praying *"continually"* (Acts 6:4). Rest assured, they were not coming before God in doubt and unbelief. No, they were fully persuaded the Lord was moving in their situation—so much so that when the seven men were appointed to minister to the widows, here's what the apostles did: *"...and when they had prayed, they laid their hands on them"* (Acts 6:6). Notice, they prayed *first!*

DISCOVER GOD'S VISION

In our fast-paced, cyber-driven life, prayer is never old-fashioned or outdated. It's not an activity we can take for granted for any reason. More than ever, this world desperately needs prayer.

If, by default, you forfeit the power of God which is available to the believer through prayer, you will never experience what the Lord desires for your future. God has a specific vision just for you, however, if you aren't in touch with Him, how will you ever know what it is?

THEY POSSESSED PRAYER POWER

From cover to cover, God's Word documents the awesome power of prayer:

- Abraham possessed prayer power: *"So Abraham prayed unto God: and God healed Abimelech, and his wife, and his maidservants; and they bare children"* (Genesis 20:17).
- Moses possessed prayer power: In the wilderness, *"...when Moses prayed unto the Lord, the fire was quenched"* (Numbers 11:2).
- Elisha possessed prayer power: *"And Elisha prayed, and said, Lord...open his eyes, that he may see. And the Lord opened the eyes of the young man; and he saw: and, behold, the mountain was full of horses and chariots of fire round about Elisha"* (2 Kings 6:17).
- Jabez possessed prayer power: *"And Jabez called on the God of Israel, saying, Oh that thou wouldest bless me indeed, and enlarge my coast, and that thine hand might be with*

41

me, and that thou wouldest keep me from evil, that it may not grieve me! And God granted him that which he requested" (1 Chronicles 4:10).

■ Jesus possessed prayer power: *"And it came to pass in those days, that he went out into a mountain to pray, and continued all night in prayer to God. And when it was day, he called unto him his disciples: and of them he chose twelve, whom also he named apostles"* (Luke 6:12-13).

■ Paul possessed prayer power: *"And it came to pass, that the father of Publius lay sick of a fever and of a bloody flux: to whom Paul entered in, and prayed, and laid his hands on him, and healed him"* (Acts 28:8).

What about you? If the book of Acts were being written today, would it include your story of how the Lord answered your heart's cry?

SEARCHING FOR THE ANSWER

As children, many of us heard the dramatic account of Daniel in the lion's den. But as we read his story, this man who was wonderfully used by God had a secret weapon he used on a daily basis. It was "prayer power."

Allow me to set the scene. King Nebuchadnezzar was baffled by a personal problem. He had a dream that he wanted interpreted—feeling the true meaning was directly tied to the future of his kingdom.

The king grew so anxious to uncover the answer to this dream that he called the astrologers, magicians and soothsayers from throughout the land for the answer. But they were unable to interpret the dream.

The situation was so troubling to the king he *"...commanded to destroy all the wise men of Babylon. And the decree went forth that the wise men should be slain; and they sought Daniel and his fellows to be slain"* (Daniel 2:12-13).

Remember, when Nebuchadnezzer overran Israel, he took four Jewish boys back with him to Babylon to be trained as advisors to the royal court. The four young men were Daniel, Shadrach, Meshach and Abednego.

"I CAN SOLVE YOUR PROBLEM"

Looking at the wise men from the king's point of view, he rationalized, "I am paying you men a great salary and honoring you. So if you can't help me when I need it most, you're fired!"

However, Daniel spoke up and said, "I can solve your problem." The Bible records, he *"...answered with counsel and wisdom to Arioch the captain of the king's guard, which was gone forth to slay the wise men of Babylon: He answered and said to Arioch the king's captain, Why is the decree so hasty from the king?* (Daniel 2:14-15).

Next, Daniel personally came before the king and promised if he would give him time, he would reveal the interpretation.

Immediately, *"Daniel went to his house, and made the thing known to...his companions: that they would desire mercies of the God of heaven concerning this secret"*(vv.17-18). In other words, they prayed!

The Bible tells us, *"Then was the secret revealed unto Daniel in a night vision. Then Daniel blessed the God of heaven. Daniel answered and said, Blessed be the name of God for ever and ever: for wisdom and might are his"*(vv.19-20).

BELIEVE FOR THE SOLUTION

When the Lord made the meaning clear, Daniel exclaimed, *"I thank thee, and praise thee, O thou God of my fathers, who hast given me wisdom and might, and hast made known unto me now what we desired of thee: for thou hast now made known unto us the king's matter"* (v.23).

Even before the Almighty answered, Daniel knew in his heart that God would respond to his plea. Remember, the Lord *"...knoweth what things ye have need of, before ye ask him"* (Matthew 6:8).

Do you have this same peace and assurance?

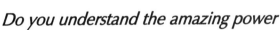

Do you understand the amazing power which is available to you?

Are you totally convinced that any circumstance or situation can be dramatically changed through prayer?

This is not something just to know or think about. You have to believe it is the solution for Satan's pollution! God has given you power which can overturn the devil's plans.

THIRTEEN ASSURANCES

There were thirteen specifics Daniel knew and believed before he prayed:

1. The answer could not come from man (Daniel 2:18).
2. Wisdom and might are God's (v.20).
3. God changes the times and seasons (v.21).
4. God removes kings and appoints kings (v.21).
5. God gives wisdom to the wise (v.21).
6. God gives knowledge to them that know understanding (v.21).
7. God reveals the deep and secret things (v.22).
8. God knows what is in the darkness (v:22).
9. The light dwells with God (v.22).
10. He knew God would give *him* wisdom and might (v23).
11. He knew God would make known unto him what he desired (v.23).
12. God's secrets would be revealed through prayer—including the king's dream (v.23).
13. Daniel knew nothing was greater than his prayers to God (Daniel 6:10,22).

FROM YOUR HEART!

At this very moment, a loving Heavenly Father is patiently waiting to hear from you. *"For the eyes of the Lord are over the righteous, and his ears are open unto their prayers"* (1 Peter 3:12).

God is not demanding or expecting words of eloquence or speech designed to impress others.

Jesus warned, *"...when thou prayest, thou shalt not be as the hypocrites are: for they love to pray standing in the synagogues and in the corners of the streets, that they may be seen of men. Verily I say unto you, They have their reward"* (Matthew 6:5).

And the Lord is not looking for *"vain repetitions"* (v.7) of hollow words or phrases. Rather, the Almighty desires for you to get alone with Him and pour out your innermost thoughts. *"But thou, when thou prayest, enter into thy closet, and when thou hast shut thy door, pray to thy Father which is in secret; and thy Father which seeth in secret shall reward thee openly"* (v.6).

THE KING WAS STUNNED!

Daniel's prayer produced powerful results! Standing before the king, he spoke this bold witness for the Great Jehovah: *"The secret which the king hath demanded cannot the wise men, the astrologers, the magicians, the soothsayers, show unto the king; but there is a God in heaven that revealeth secrets, and maketh known to the king Nebuchadnezzar what shall be in the latter days"* (Daniel 2:27-28).

Daniel informed the king that his dream was of a huge statue that was smashed to bits by a large stone which became a mountain. The pieces of the broken statue represented the coming kingdoms which would all be demolished. Then Daniel added, *"And in the days of these kings shall the God of heaven set up a kingdom, which shall never be destroyed...and shall stand forever"* (v.44).

King Nebuchadnezzar was stunned! At that moment, he fell on his face before Daniel and declared, *"Of a truth it is, that your God is a God of gods, and a Lord of kings, and a revealer of secrets, seeing thou couldest reveal this secret"* (v.47).

The grateful ruler promoted Daniel, lavished him with gifts and made him governor over Babylon.

Oh, what prayer can do!

A Prayer Away!

Some people argue, "If God is sovereign, why would He ask us to pray. What difference could it possibly make if He already knows the outcome?

Friend, God desires to work through His children to manifest what is best for people on this earth. This is why He asks us to pray, *"Thy will be done in earth, as it is in heaven"* (Matthew 6:10).

I know there are no sick people in heaven, so I'm to pray for the sick here on earth. I know there are no poor people in heaven, so I'm to pray for total provision and continual supply for those around me.

Does talking with God really make a difference? I can tell you from personal experience it does. The Bible says, *"...ye have not, because ye ask not"* (James 4:2).

Today, you too can experience God's wonder-working power. It's only a prayer away.

CHAPTER 4

IS GOD LISTENING?

The power of your prayer life is basically determined by the strength of your believing and the degree of your boldness as you approach God. We need to ask ourselves, "How strongly do I believe what I am asking the Lord for?

One morning, during the early days of my walk with God, I was praying and worshiping, yet failed to seek Him for a particular need—because I was trying to find the answer myself. Then, clearly, I heard the voice of the Lord say, "Why don't you ask Me to do this for you?"

It was like a eureka moment. I wondered, "Why didn't I think of that?" And the Lord replied, "Because you didn't believe."

For many, it doesn't even cross their minds to ask

for God's help. Unconsciously, we try to solve problems for ourselves.

Years ago, when I was working in a secular job, I was praying when the Lord whispered, "Why don't you ask Me for a raise or promotion?"

Sure, I had thought how nice it would be to have a better income, but I didn't think to bother the Lord. But when I addressed the issue in the spiritual, I was blessed in the natural.

As I grew in faith, I became bold in my requests to God Almighty.

ASKING "AMISS"?

You may be facing a monumental problem, but if you fail to ask in faith, your words will never make it to heaven. It's what the Bible calls asking "amiss."

James writes, *"From whence come wars and fightings among you? come they not hence, even of your lusts that war in your members? Ye lust, and have not: ye kill, and desire to have, and cannot obtain: ye fight and war, yet ye have not, because ye ask not. Ye ask, and receive not, because ye ask amiss, that ye may consume it upon your lusts"* (James 4:1-2).

While you may be asking, it is with unbelief.

When you are consumed with circumstances, feelings and your flesh, it's like picking up a shotgun and blindly firing away without aiming at your target.

This is why James counsels, *"If any of you lack wisdom, let him ask of God, that giveth to all men liberally, and upbraideth not; and it shall be given him. But let him ask in faith, nothing wavering. For he that wavereth is like a wave of the sea driven with the wind and tossed"* (James 1:5-6).

———— ❦ ————

What's the secret to receiving wisdom? "Ask in faith."

REMOVE THE CLUTTER!

Your pastor may agree with you for your prayers to be answered, whether it involves your career, your health, your finances or your family. But does he really know your spiritual depth?

Who knows, you may be a workaholic, choose to spend all day on the Internet, or talk incessantly with friends on the phone—day after day, week after week, month after month. Yet, you complain, "I don't have time to pray."

James tells us to talk to God in faith, *"nothing wavering."* To reach this objective we must remove the clutter which chokes our lives and with total faith enter the Throne Room of Heaven. Otherwise, *"Let not that man think that he shall receive anything of the Lord. A double minded man is unstable in all his ways"* (vv.7-8)."

———————— ❦ ————————

**How can you receive God's favor
if you ask in unbelief?**

As you become spiritually stronger by applying these principles, your belief will mature to the point you will be able to say without hesitation, "I *know* God will answer my prayer."

"THAT TINGLING SENSATION"

As believers, we understand the Lord is able, but is His power active and working inside us? Paul writes, *"Now unto him that is able to do exceeding abundantly above all that we ask or think, according to the power that worketh in us"* (Ephesians 3:20),

If something is functioning properly, its action is dynamic. Perhaps you are old enough to remember the old Alka-Seltzer™ commercial where they dropped two tablets in a glass of water to the theme, "Plop, Plop, Fizz, Fizz, oh what a relief it is!"

Wow! That was powerful advertizing—because you could visualize how this product could work for you.

Or perhaps you've seen a promo for Selsun Blue™ shampoo with a model's hair lathered in foam, while the announcer says, "That tingling sensation means its working!"

Well, according to the Father, His power is at work in us—as the result of believing. Unfortunately, our prayers often lack luster; there is no "bubbly effervescence."

Personally, I know when I have reached a certain intensity or strength in my belief and it becomes dynamic. I say to myself, "Yeah! This is going to work! Faith has arrived!

PLUG INTO THE POWER

I love Ephesians 3:20 in the Amplified Bible: *"Now to Him Who, by* (in consequence of) *the* [action of His] *power that is at work within us, is able to* [carry out His purpose and] *do superabundantly, far over and above all that we* [dare] *ask or think* [infinitely beyond our highest prayers, desires, thoughts, hopes, or dreams]."

To give a physical example, a building has electricity terminating at outlets. These outlets are specifically designed and installed for you to insert a plug and make a demand on the available power. So your ability to receive the electricity is based upon the strength of your decision to insert the plug. It's not about the power, rather your choice.

Spiritually, answers to prayer do not just concern God's ability to act on your behalf; it is about how confident you are to say, "Do I dare ask the Lord for this?"

I've heard people comment, "God doesn't want you to have this. It is not His will for you" —as if the Lord is the problem. Or, they imply, "You have to do something to impress Him to make this happen."

In truth, to be in spiritual alignment, we only need to believe what the Word declares God will do.

FULLY PERSUADED

Let's look at the life of Abraham. The reason he heard from God is because he believed. *"(As it is written, I have made thee a father of many nations,) before him whom he believed, even God, who quickeneth the dead, and calleth those things which be not as though they were."* (Romans 4:17).

Abraham knew that (1) God raises the dead and (2) the Almighty speaks life. As a result, *"He staggered not at the promise of God through unbelief; but was strong in faith, giving glory to God; And being fully per-suaded that, what he had promised, he was able also to perform"* (vv.20-21).

The lesson is, if you need to grow strong in your asking, get to truly know the One to whom you are praying.

It was not just Abraham who believed, but also Sarah. *"Through faith also Sara herself received strength to conceive seed, and was delivered of a child when she was past age, because she judged him faithful who had promised"* (Hebrews 11:11).

By believing the Creator was a God of His Word, she received strength to bear a child in her old age.

HE KNEW GOD'S LOVE

When others turned toward the wicked city of Sodom, *"Abraham stood yet before the Lord"*(Genesis 18:22). He came near to God and asked, *"Wilt thou also destroy the righteous with the wicked? Peradventure there be fifty righteous within the city: wilt thou also destroy and not spare the place for the fifty righteous that are therein?"* (vv.23-24).

Notice what Abraham stated next: *"That be far from thee to do after this manner, to slay the righteous with the wicked"*(v.25).

How did he know this about God? The sins of Sodom were not his reference point, Abraham was praying with the Father's love and righteousness in mind.

GOD'S SOLUTION, NOT OURS

Intercession requires that we understand God's love and forgiveness rather than focusing on the sins committed by an individual—whether drugs, theft or adultery. The Lord loves the person regardless of their mistakes and failures, and you should too. Simply come before God on their behalf, knowing the Father desires a solution even more than you. Remember,

"The Lord is not slack concerning his promise, as some men count slackness; but is longsuffering to us-ward, not willing that any should perish, but that all should come to repentance" (2 Peter 3:9).

Even if the sinner is running from God and resents your concern, intercede for them anyway—otherwise they could be left without hope. Jesus says, *"Love your enemies, bless them that curse you, do good to them that hate you, and pray for them which despitefully use you, and persecute you"* (Matthew 5:44).

How do you pray for people who are incarcerated for crimes of murder, rape or tax embezzlement. How will you reach them?

My friend, you need to know about God's unfailing love and compassion, not just the sad details of a person's failures.

SAVED BY GRACE

In the case of Sodom, Abraham knew the Almighty would not destroy the righteous with the wicked, so he continued questioning God: *"Peradventure there shall be forty* [righteous] *found there. And he said, I will not do it for forty's sake"* (Genesis 18:29).

Abraham kept lowering the number—thirty, twenty, ten—and finally God said He would not destroy the city for ten righteous (v.32). So after Lot and his family were safely outside the walls of Sodom, it was totally annihilated.

In the final analysis, God is looking for those who are willing to be saved by His grace.

A NEW DAY

During the ministry of Jesus, one day in Jerusalem He was walking with His disciples and *"saw a man which was blind from his birth"* (John 9:1).

The disciples turned to Him and asked, *"Master, who did sin, this man, or his parents, that he was born blind?"* (v.2).

Jesus answered, *"Neither had this man sinned nor his parents: but that the works of God should be made manifest in him"* (v.3).

In Jewish tradition, either the sins of the fathers or

some personal iniquity must have caused this condition.

Jesus was letting them know a new era had dawned and the past was the past. He declared, *"I must work the works of him that sent me, while it is day: the night cometh, when no man can work. As long as I am in the world, I am the light of the world"* (vv.4-5).

Next, the Son of God spat on the ground, made clay of the spittle and used it to anoint the eyes of the blind man. Jesus told him to wash his eyes in the pool of Siolam and when he did, the man came back healed (v.7).

"I WAS BLIND— NOW I SEE!"

As you can imagine, the news of this awesome miracle spread quickly and the man was brought to the Pharisees to give his testimony of healing. This set off a firestorm, not because of the miracle, but the fact Jesus did this on the Sabbath.

There was much consternation among the Pharisees. Some argued, *"This man is not of God, because he keepeth not the sabbath day. Others said, How can a man that is a sinner do such miracles?"* (v.16).

Once more, *they called the man who was blind and*

said to him, *"Give God the praise: we know that this man* [Jesus] *is a sinner. He answered and said, Whether he be a sinner or no, I know not: one thing I know, that, whereas I was blind, now I see"* (vv.24-25). Then the former sightless man looked at the religious critics and said, *"...will ye also be his disciples?"* (v.27).

Wow! They didn't like this one bit! But when God touches your life you suddenly have His courage and it makes no difference what others think.

All the Pharisees could answer was that they were disciples of Moses, but didn't know where this Jesus came from.

The healed man, however, commented, *"...herein is a marvelous thing, that ye know not from whence he is, and yet he hath opened mine eyes. Now we know that God heareth not sinners: but if any man be a worshipper of God, and doeth his will, him he heareth. Since the world began was it not heard that any man opened the eyes of one that was born blind. If this man were not of God, he could do nothing"* (vv.30-33).

This former blind man became knowledgeable of spiritual matters in a hurry. He was talking with theologians and beating them at their own game.

The pharisees didn't like his attitude and threw him out in the street (v.34). "Who do you think you are?" they scoffed.

When I read this story many years ago I thought, "Why should I ever conclude God doesn't hear me when I pray? I am no longer a sinner. I'm born again!"

Never allow doubt to sabotage the effectiveness of your prayer life.

IT WORKS!

Is God listening when you call on Him? According to Scripture the answer is an emphatic "Yes!" As the psalmist writes, *"I love the Lord, because he hath heard my voice and my supplications. Because he hath inclined his ear unto me, therefore will I call upon him as long as I live"* (Psalm 116:1-2).

This is a powerful statement because the psalmist is declaring, "When something works, I'm going to keep doing it. I will continue calling on God."

In today's world you don't keep using credit cards

ANDRÉ GORHAM

once they are maxed out—and you can't keep driving when you run out of gas. But if all signals are "Go" you keep moving forward.

Well, since God answers prayer, why stop calling on Him?

ONE DAY AT A TIME?

When I first became a believer I didn't know you could make a lifetime commitment to God, because the people around me would make statements such as, "One day at a time, sweet Jesus." It was almost like they were afraid to commit to Him for a week or more because they didn't know what was going to happen. There also seemed to be a fear of backsliding.

I even knew individuals who wouldn't dedicate their lives to the Lord because they felt they would fail and didn't want to be called hypocrites.

———— ❦ ————

Salvation takes place in a moment of time, but developing your spiritual life is a process.

HE HEARS AND ANSWERS

If you ever enter into a conversation with a person

who doesn't believe God hears them when they pray, share these verses:

- *"I sought the Lord, and he heard me, and delivered me from all my fears"* (Psalm 34:4).

- *"The righteous cry, and the Lord heareth, and delivereth them out of all their troubles"* (Psalm 34:17).

- *"For the eyes of the Lord are over the righteous, and his ears are open unto their prayers"* (1 Peter 3:12).

- *"Thou hast given him his heart's desire, and hast not withholden the request of his lips"* (Psalm 21:2).

- *"But know that the Lord hath set apart him that is godly for himself: the Lord will hear when I call unto him"* (Psalm 4:3).

- *"My voice shalt thou hear in the morning, O Lord; in the morning will I direct my prayer unto thee"* (Psalm 5:3).

- *"Lord, thou hast heard the desire of the humble: thou wilt prepare their heart, thou wilt cause thine ear to hear"* (Psalm 10:17).

- *"Now know I that the Lord saveth his anointed; he will hear him from his holy heaven with the saving strength of his right hand"* (Psalm 20:6).

- *"As for me, I will call upon God; and the Lord shall save me. Evening, and morning, and at noon, will I pray, and cry aloud: and he shall hear my voice"* (Psalm 55:16-17).

- *"I cried unto the Lord with my voice, and he heard me out of his holy hill"* (Psalm 3:4).

- *"The Lord hath heard my supplication; the Lord will receive my prayer"* (Psalm 6:9).

- *"I waited patiently for the Lord; and he inclined unto me, and heard my cry. He brought me up also out of an horrible pit, out*

*of the miry clay, and set my feet upon a rock,
and established my goings"* (Psalm 40:1-2).

■ *"And whatsoever we ask, we receive of him,
because we keep his commandments, and do
those things that are pleasing in his sight"*
(1 John 3:22).

■ *"And this is the confidence that we have in
him, that, if we ask any thing according to his
will, he heareth us: And if we know that he
hear us, whatsoever we ask, we know that we
have the petitions that we desired of him"*
(1 John 5:14-15).

Is God listening? Take His Word for it, He is—and
even more important, He is ready to answer your
prayers.

67

CHAPTER 5

SIX CHARACTERISTICS OF PEOPLE WHO SUCCEED IN PRAYER

What makes the defining difference between a believer who is hearing from heaven almost daily and one who never seems to have anything to praise God for?

Considering this question led me to what I want to share with you now—six important characteristics of people who succeed in prayer.

After studying the Scriptures detailing these qualities, make it your aim to have each one operating in your life. If just one is missing, it will affect the results you desire from the Lord.

From time to time, review this list to make sure you maintain a balanced approach to a faith-filled, Spirit-blessed walk with God

What characteristics do achievers in prayer possess?

1. They have an intimate knowledge of the Word and will of God concerning the thing about which they are praying.

When you come before the Lord, it is absolutely essential that you know God's will related to your petitions. For example, if you are approaching the Lord regarding your health, totally believe what the Word declares concerning your physical body: *"I am the Lord that healeth thee"* (Exodus 15:26). *"Bless the Lord, O my soul, and forget not all his benefits: Who forgiveth all thine iniquities; who healeth all thy diseases"* (Psalm 103:2-3).

Remember, God only hears us if we ask "according to his will" (1 John 5:14).

In the Old Testament we find a prime example of a person who stood firmly on God's Word—and was able to pray the will of the Almighty to achieve victory. His name was Jehoshaphat, king of Judah.

When news arrived that the Moabites and Ammonites had joined forces to make war on his kingdom, Jehoshaphat *"set himself to seek the Lord and proclaimed a fast throughout all Judah"* (2 Chronicles 20:3).

Standing before the assembled nation in the temple at Jerusalem, He prayed, *"O Lord God of our fathers, art not thou God in heaven? and rulest not thou over all the kingdoms of the heathen? and in thine hand is there not power and might, so that none is able to withstand thee? Art not thou our God, who didst drive out the inhabitants of this land before thy people Israel, and gavest it to the seed of Abraham thy friend for ever? And they dwelt therein, and have built thee a sanctuary therein for thy name, saying, If, when evil cometh upon us, as the sword, judgment, or pestilence, or famine, we stand before this house, and in thy presence, (for thy name is in this house,) and cry unto thee in our affliction, then thou wilt hear and help"* (2 Chronicles 20:6-10).

This testifies to the fact Jehoshaphat was familiar with the Word and how it related to answering this specific prayer. But now he is reminding the nation and God Himself concerning the matter.

Regarding the threat by the invading armies, he acknowledged his total dependance on the Lord—*"...for we have no might against this great*

71

company that cometh against us; neither know we what to do: but our eyes are upon thee" (v.12).

When the people were ready to march into battle, the king proclaimed, *"Believe in the Lord your God, so shall ye be established; believe his prophets, so shall ye prosper"* (v.20).

Next, Jehoshaphat appointed a choir to march ahead of the troops, singing, *"Praise the Lord; for his mercy endureth forever"*(v.21).

As soon as the people began singing and praising, God *"set ambushments"* against the invading armies (v.22). Scripture records how the men of Ammon, Moab and Mount Sier became so confused they actually attacked and killed each other (vv.22-23).

This entire process of events took place because Jehoshaphat had an intimate knowledge of God's Word and His will.

Remember, *"the world passeth away...but he that doeth the will of God abideth forever"*(1 John 2:17),

2. They are diligent in their prayers.

There are only two people mentioned in the Bible who were physically taken up into heaven: Elijah and Enoch. *"By faith Enoch was translated that he should not see death; and was not found, because God had translated him: for before his translation he had this testimony, that he pleased God. But without faith it is impossible to please him: for he that cometh to God must believe that he is, and that he is a rewarder of them that diligently seek him"* (Hebrews 11:5-6).

Diligently praying for God to intervene in a situation—such as the restoration of a fractured marriage—is different than just *hoping* for something to change. This is the kind of persevering prayer the Lord rewards.

God is looking for certain qualities to be evident in your Christian walk.

Peter counsels, *"...giving all diligence, add to your faith virtue; and to virtue knowledge; and to knowledge temperance; and to temperance patience; and to patience godliness; and to godliness brotherly kindness; and to brotherly kindness charity. For if these things be in you, and abound, they make you that ye shall neither be barren nor unfruitful in the knowledge of our Lord Jesus Christ"* (2 Peter 1:5-8).

Then Peter adds, *"...give diligence to make your*

calling and election sure: for if ye do these things, ye shall never fall" (v.10).

Are you conscientious, earnest and energetic in approaching God?

The Bible tells us, *"Keep thy heart with all diligence; for out of it are the issues of life"* (Proverbs 4:23).

3. They pray with determination.

In the city of Tyre, on the southern coast of what is now Lebanon, Jesus entered a house where He thought He would not be recognized. But just as He entered, a Greek woman (Syro-Phoenician by birth), heard where He was. She fell at the Lord's feet, begging for help, asking Him to cure her demon possessed child.

His answer seemed rather abrupt. Jesus said, *"Let the children first be filled: for it is not meet to take the children's bread, and to cast it unto the dogs"* (Mark 7:27).

She thoughtfully replied, "Of course, Master. But don't the dogs under the table at least get the scraps dropped by the children?"

Here was a woman who refused to be pushed aside. She firmly stood her ground.

Jesus' response to this woman's determination was: *"For this saying go thy way; the devil is gone out of thy daughter"* (v.29).

She went home and found her daughter completely set free. The demon was gone out of her!

"I WILL NOT BE DENIED!"

On another occasion, Jesus shared a parable illustrating it is necessary for us to pray continually, never giving up (Luke 18:1).

The story concerned a judge who gave no thought or respect to God—and cared even less for people. A widow in his jurisdiction who felt her rights were being violated, said, *"Avenge me of mine adversary"* (v.3).

For a while he did nothing. But because the widow troubled him, he said he would avenge her.

The woman's sheer persistence produced results.

To this the Lord commented, *"Hear what the unjust judge saith. And shall not God avenge his own elect, which cry day and night unto him, though he bear long with them? I tell you that he will avenge them speedily"* (vv.6-8).

Are you at the place where you can declare, "I will not be denied! I am determined to receive these things from God—no matter what!"

4. They pray aggressively.

People who are slipshod and lazy, praying when the mood hits them, will not be successful with God. You need to be aggressive—to go after what you want. Reclining in an armchair, waiting for the skies to open and drop answers on a silver platter, is not the route to take.

Yes, God will answer, but there needs to be a certain spiritual hunger involved.

By "aggression," I am not referring to the physical, but in your prayer time, the Lord expects you to be assertive.

Remember, the weapons of your warfare are not carnal; they are mighty through God to the pulling down of strongholds (2 Corinthians 10:4).

Scripture tells us, *"And from the days of John the Baptist until now the kingdom of heaven suffereth violence, and the violent take it by force"* (Matthew 11:12).

If you do not resist, rebuke and cast out the devil, he will continue his devious plans. But when you face him head-on and demand, *"Get thee behind me, Satan"* (Matthew 16:23), he gets the message and takes off running!

HE WOULDN'T LET GO

Isaac's son, Jacob, is a perfect example of spiritual aggressiveness. During a journey he wrestled all night with an angel and wouldn't surrender. The angel finally pleaded, *"Let me go, for the day breaketh"* (Genesis 32:26).

Jacob replied, *"I will not let thee go, except thou bless me"* (v.26).

The angel asked, "What is your name?" And he replied, "Jacob."

To this, the angel announced, *"Thy name shall be called no more Jacob, but Israel: for as a prince hast thou power with God and with men, and hast prevailed"* (v.28).

After the angel blessed him, Jacob called the name of the place Peniel, which means: *"for I have seen God face to face, and my life is preserved"* (v.30).

How serious are you about receiving your answer from the Lord? Do you regularly set aside time to pray, even if it means an all night session on your knees?

Personally, once I find out the will of God, I pray with every fibre of my being. I thank the Lord, praise and worship Him and wrap words around the request of my heart.

I believe what I achieve spiritually is far more important than what I will eventually do physically. I know that faith without works is dead—but works without faith is also dead!

PRAYER THAT GETS RESULTS

My second son was born with a chronic lung disease. He had severe asthma and breathing problems. Furthermore, the doctor said he would have this condition all his life.

Although great medical practitioners were working on my son, I also had Jesus the Great Physician. I spoke the Word, praised, worshiped and thanked God in advance for what He was about to do. I declared, "Father, you are the Healer and Deliverer. Thank You for performing a miracle for my child."

I repeated these words morning, noon and night, every day for about 20 days. This wasn't a hardship, because I knew if I didn't continue thanking God for the victory, I would lose my son.

At the same time, the doctors were telling me that even if he lived, he would likely have brain damage and other medical problems.

This has been many years ago, and with a spirit of thanksgiving I can testify that my son has no mental damage or breathing problems. He is also very strong academically.

*Believe me when I tell you, aggressive
prayer produces results.*

5. They are patient with God.

Patience is the time element between when you pray and when the manifestation arrives—whether it is one second, one hour, one month, one year, or even a decade.

We are counseled to *"be not slothful, but followers of them who through faith and patience inherit the promises.* "(Hebrews 6:12).

Scripture is referring to God's pledge to Abraham: *"Surely blessing I will bless thee, and multiplying I will multiply thee. And so, after he had patiently endured, he obtained the promise"* (vv.14-15).

Did the answer come instantly? No, but Abraham eventually received everything he had been assured of —and even more!

———— 🪶 ————

The principle of waiting on God is a continual theme of Scripture.

We are told, *"Cast not away therefore your confidence, which hath great recompense of reward. For ye have need of patience, that, after ye have done the will of God, ye might receive the promise"* (Hebrews 10:35-36).

In this case, the promise is Christ's return: *"For yet a little while, and he that shall come will come, and will not tarry"* (v.37).

The apostle James reminds us if we lack the virtue of patience, we can receive it by doing things God's way: *"Knowing this, that the trying of your faith worketh patience. But let patience have her perfect work, that ye may be perfect and entire, wanting nothing"* (James 1:3-4).

This doesn't say the testing of your money or your marriage, but the *"trying of your faith"*—your confession based on the Word.

Patience is also key to receiving wisdom, knowledge and understanding. Paul writes, *"For whatsoever things were written aforetime were written for our learning, that we through patience and comfort of the scriptures might have hope"* (Romans 15:4).

Every time I open the Holy book there is much to discover. I learn how to avoid what Samuel, David and Samson went through, but also how to become a victorious overcomer through Christ.

6. They trust God instead of man.

Instead of placing my confidence in the almighty dollar, I choose to live by what is written on it: "In God We Trust."

I rely upon prayer to accomplish what doctors, lawyers, accountants or politicians can never provide. By simple belief, it gives me instant access to the Father in the name of Jesus Christ.

As a result of fellowship with God, I know the Holy Spirit is working on my behalf and even angels are watching over me.

I'll admit there was a time in my life when I was ambivalent concerning prayer—and could take it or leave it. This was before I began to attend a church where the Word was paramount. Then, as I began to incorporate and implement Scripture into my Christianity, my spiritual life zoomed into orbit.

One day I exclaimed, "Wow! This really works!"

Here's the best part. What God does once, He will do again. It's more mathematically exact than science and more precise than geometry.

WHERE IS YOUR TRUST?

I have studied many great books, but there is none to compare with God's Word. It is alive—and every time I open its pages I find nuggets of truth just for me.

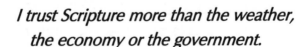

I trust Scripture more than the weather,
the economy or the government.

Where do you place your hope? Is it in an academic degree, an inheritance or some earthly resource? These are temporal and will one day fade away. David writes, *"Some trust in chariots, and some in horses: but we will remember the name of the Lord our God"* (Psalm 20:7).

The apostle Paul offers this sound advice: *"Charge them that are rich in this world, that they be not highminded, nor trust in uncertain riches, but in the living God, who giveth us richly all things to enjoy"* (1 Timothy 6:17).

Make certain your communion with God incorporates these six characteristics: (1) knowledge of the Word, (2) diligence, (3) determination, (4) aggressiveness, (5) patience and (6) trust. If it does, on the authority of Scripture, you will succeed in prayer.

CHAPTER 6

YOUR PRAYER QUESTIONS ANSWERED

Communicating with God is one of the most cherished aspects of our Christian journey. Yet, as we fellowship with an unseen Father there are always questions: What words should I use? What part do ministering angels play? What preparations should I make before approaching God?—and many more.

Let me share a few answers:

What is prayer?

Prayer is a dedicated, focused believing toward God about a specific person, place or thing. The primary emphasis, however, must be on the Lord—and by pleasing Him we will receive a divine response.

(Numbers 14:6-9; Proverbs 16:7; 1 John 3:22; Psalm 34:3-10).

Prayer is God and you working together to have His heavenly involvement in earthly matters (2 Chronicles 7:14).

We should expand our definition to include what prayer is *not*:

- Prayer is not meditation, though these sometimes work together (Psalm 19:14; Genesis 24:63; Joshua 1:8).
- Prayer is not confessions or declarations of faith (Job 22:28; Mark 11:24; Hebrews 10:23).
- Prayer is not thinking to oneself.
- Prayer is not praise, even though they may occur together (Acts 16:25; Daniel 2:23).
- Prayer is not thanksgiving, although it should be combined with prayer (Daniel 6:10-11; Philippians 4:6).
- Pray is not worry.
- Prayer is not cries of desperation though when you pray you may be desperate (Luke 18:1-10; Daniel 6:1-11).

It is faith and belief that move the hand of God.

What is the source and constitution of real prayer?

The center of prayer is the heart and it consists of:

- A specific and precise desire (Mark 11:24).
- A strong belief in God's help in the matter for which you are praying (2 Chronicles 20:3-12; Psalm 46:1; Psalm 121:1; Hebrews 4:16).
- The acute recognition that the issue is beyond you, your resources and abilities (2 Corinthians 12:9-10; 2 Chronicles 20:12).
- It is always directed toward God, not toward the need for the situation to change (Ephesians 3:14,20; Psalm 2:8; 2 Chronicles 32:18-20).

We can approach the Father with authority and confidence because:

- He deeply loves and cares for us (John 16:26-27).
- We have the faith of Jesus (2 Corinthians 4:13; Ephesians 2:18; Ephesians 3:12).
- We are His children (Galatians 4:1-7).

- We have the blood of Jesus (Hebrews 10:19).
- We have a High Priest who is between us and our God (Hebrews 4:14-16; Hebrews 10:21-23).

Prayer is not just asking, rather the context in which asking occurs.

It is a posture, a position and an inward place of believing where requests, petitions and desires toward God take place (Psalm 2:8). Remember, Jesus says, *"And all things, whatsoever ye shall ask in prayer, believing, ye shall receive"* (Matthew 21:22).

The "ask in prayer" is the posture or context.

What is meant by a "secret place"?

The psalmist writes, *"He that dwelleth in the secret place of the most High shall abide under the shadow of the Almighty"* (Psalm 91:1).

There is a divine connection between heaven and earth. It is called the "secret place." You will discover more about this "secret place" in prayer.

In the New Testament, Jesus tells us to enter into our closet to pray to God—*"and thy Father which seeth in secret shall reward thee openly"* (Matthew 6:6).

The closet refers to a physical place, however, God *"seeth in secret."* This gives us a unique insight into how the Lord works. As Jesus taught on prayer and fasting, He spoke of the Father *"which is in secret"* (v.6) rewarding us.

Furthermore, Colossians 3:1-2 tells us to *"seek those things which are above"* and how we should set our affection *"on things above."* So this secret place is not just some inward void of nothingness; it relates to "above."

As we turn to the last book in the New Testament, Revelation, we can find the location where all this is taking place. The *"four and twenty elders fell down before the Lamb, having every one of them harps, and golden vials full of odours, which are the prayers of saints"* (Revelation 5:8).

Our prayers from the "secret place" are received in Heaven. We also know the *"smoke of the incense, which came with the prayers of the saints, ascended up before God"* (Revelation 8:4).

What preparations should I make for prayer?

Before asking God for a specific need, prepare your heart by studying Scriptures which relate to your situation. This will help you develop a capacity for faith concerning what you want the Father to accomplish (Hebrews 11:6).

Also, address and deal with any sin in your life (1 John 1:9).

Please examine your heart for fear, unbelief and unforgiveness (Psalm 66:17-20; Mark 11:25-26; 1 John 3:19-21; 1Chronicles 29:16-19; Ezra 7:10; 2 Chronicles 11:16; 12:14; 19:3, 30:19).

We must remember, all believing is birthed in the heart. If there is a deficiency in this area it will greatly affect your ability to believe and receive from God (Proverbs 18:14; 1 Peter 3:7).

First John 3:19-22 declares, *"And hereby we know that we are of the truth, and shall assure our hearts before him. For if our heart condemn us, God is greater than our heart, and knoweth all things. Beloved, if our heart condemn us not, then have we confidence toward God. And whatsoever we ask, we receive of him, because we keep his commandments, and do those things that are pleasing in his sight."*

Ask yourself:

- What do I want or need God to do for me?
- Do I believe the Lord will answer in this specific request?

- What Scriptures support my desire?
- Do I believe this can be accomplished by prayer alone? (Matthew 26: 53).

We must be honest with ourselves regarding how much knowledge we possess about God, the Word and His will for our lives (please read Luke 14:28-33).

An awareness of where we are in
our spiritual journey will keep us from
being frustrated in our prayer lives.

God declares, *"My people are destroyed for lack of knowledge"* (Hosea 4:6).

Unfortunately, I have seen some believers attempt to achieve significant results with only minimal dedication. More is required. First, we need to greatly feed our faith and Bible commitment.

When you study the book of Job you will find he understood certain things regarding God his three friends didn't. This lack of knowledge on Job's friends part caused them to sin with their speech, much to their own destruction (Job 42:2-9).

Consequently, it was Job who had to help them out

of their "mouth-made" afflictions: *"And the Lord turned the captivity of Job, when he prayed for his friends: also the Lord gave Job twice as much as he had before"* (v.10).

—————— ❧ ——————

Know where you are in your walk with God
—and ask for help when necessary.

Talk to people who have won or received the victory in the area of your need. Wanting the Lord to answer beyond your own spiritual limitations or beyond the ability of your local church can lead to frustration and much disappointment.

What part do angels play in prayer?

Our prayers to God release ministering spirits who are sent to assist the heirs of salvation (Hebrews 1:14; Psalm 103:20; Revelation 8:5).

In the Bible, prayer constantly involves angels (2 Chronicles 32:18-22; Daniel 6:22; 10:8-21; Matthew 26:53; Luke 22:43; Acts 10:1-7; 12:1-17).

What is the true significance of these heavenly beings? Please understand, there are invisible and evil forces behind the negative circumstances we face

(Ephesians 6:12; 2 Corinthian 10:3-7). These forces, though spiritual, work through people and physical entities (Daniel 10:12-15).

Angels, however, though unseen, operate in the invisible toward our benefit and good. They keep evil powers at bay and engage them toward our advantage as we use words of faith and prayers of belief.

Daniel 10:13 tells us the prince of the Kingdom of Persia, who was a satanic, spiritual being, tried to thwart the heavenly help which was at Daniel's disposal. This resistance of Satan required Michael, a chief angel, to assist in the matter.

We need to understand and appreciate the importance of angels as our servants and guardians (Daniel 10: 21; Hebrews 1:14).

David declares, *"The angel of the Lord encampeth round about them that fear him, and delivereth them"* (Psalm 34:7).

Hebrews 12:22 illustrates how we are *"come unto mount Sion, and unto the city of the living God, the heavenly Jerusalem, and to an innumerable company of angels."*

All great households have servants at their disposal and it is no different in the household of God (Matthew 26:53; John 18:36; Galatians 6:10; 2 Timothy 2:20).

Throughout Scripture and in our lives, angels, seen and unseen, are at work to help us. The awareness of these heavenly beings help our mindset and attitude as we pray.

We must never focus on the angels nor worship them (please read Revelation 22:8-9). Instead we should direct our prayers to our Father knowing that angels assist us as we align our lives with what God declares.

What words should we use in prayer?

When praying, say what you mean and mean what you say! Keep it simple, avoiding lofty words or phrases.

Prayer is a conversation—a dialogue between you and God (Isaiah 1:18). So let the Lord know how essential this is to you.

An angel came to Daniel and said, *"Fear not...for from the first day that thou didst set thine heart to understand, and to chasten thyself before thy God, thy words were heard, and I am come for thy words"* (Daniel 10:12).

Don't be afraid to repeat your request. Before the crucifixion, Jesus prayed to His Father, *"...not as I will, but as thou wilt"* (Matthew 26:39). Then he said it again, *"O my Father, if this cup may not pass away from me, except I drink it, thy will be done"* (v.42).

Then, when He found the disciples sleeping, Scripture records, He *"went away again, and prayed the third time, saying the same words"* (v.44).

Why was this necessary when He knew the will of God? The poignant, believing words Jesus expressed in prayer brought an angel who provided the strength He needed to accomplish the great work awaiting Him (Luke 22:43).

Never take lightly the words of your prayers. Declare with the psalmist, *"Let the words of my mouth, and the meditation of my heart, be acceptable in thy sight, O Lord, my strength, and redeemer"* (Psalm 19:14).

Is this your prayer?

CHAPTER 7

CHANGING THINGS THROUGH BELIEVING PRAYER

With God, no request is too insignificant, but I believe we can also ask for and receive what is exceptional—*"above all that we ask or think"* (Ephesians 3:20).

One of the purposes of prayer is to produce change —to move from where you are to a much more desirable place. For example, when James addresses the issue of sickness, he writes, *"Is any among you afflicted? let him pray"* (James 5:13). This suggests that praying will see your illness turn-around for the better.

In the natural world we often fall short and fail to achieve the success we are seeking, but in God's

Kingdom and according to His Word, we can call on the Lord at any time and have His victory.

The promises of the Father are not hypothetical or theoretical, they should be active in your life today. So when we examine how prayer works, we find it mends what is broken and turns the old into new.

IT'S NOT CONDITIONAL

In the New Testament we read how James calls for the elders of the church to pray over a person who is sick, *"anointing him with oil in the name of the Lord"* (James 5:14).

What will be the outcome? The *"prayer of faith shall save the sick, and the Lord shall raise him up"* (v.15).

A "faith" prayer is more than muttering, "Lord, if it be Your will," or "I hope it will happen." Such words signify unbelieving, conditional praying by a person who doesn't understand God intends for us to be healed—and the outcome will be disappointing. Weak, uncertain prayers will never produce miracles.

I find it astounding there are some believers who are convinced God's power to heal on earth ended with the disciples in the first century church—and is not applicable today.

When Jesus said, *"...these signs shall follow them that believe"* (Mark 16:17), He was referring to you and me. And one of those signs is, *"...they shall lay hands on the sick, and they shall recover"* (v.17).

Why does God bring healing? Because He responds to our faith.

STEPS OF SPIRITUAL GROWTH

As a new Christian, the Lord doesn't expect you to accomplish great feats in His name. Like any child, it takes time before you learn to walk—so you start by taking baby steps. However, as you develop spiritually through studying Scripture, seeding the Word, obeying God and living by faith, your prayer life should correspond accordingly. There should be parallel growth.

There are things I pray for today that I would never have dared to mention ten years ago. I just wasn't spiritually developed.

This was also true in the life of the disciples. For instance, after Jesus foretold He would be betrayed by one of the twelve, while He was speaking, Judas came, *"and with him a great multitude with swords and staves, from the chief priests and elders of the people"* (Matthew 26:47).

As they were taking Jesus away, Peter *"stretched out his hand, and drew his sword, and struck a servant of the high priest's, and smote off his ear"* (v.51).

Immediately, Jesus said, *"Put up again thy sword into his place: for all they that take the sword shall perish with the sword"* (v.52).

Peter, still a novice in the things of God, had much to learn concerning how to face a crisis, and the power of prayer.

Jesus told him, *"Thinkest thou that I cannot now pray to my Father, and he shall presently give me more than twelve legions of angels? But how then shall the scriptures be fulfilled, that thus it must be?"* (vv.53-54).

A legion is 6,000, and multiplied by 12 meant God would provide 72,000 angels in answer to prayer! Obviously, Jesus believed He could go to His Father for all the help He needed. Then He added, "But if I make such a request, would prophecy be fulfilled?"

How firm is your belief? In the Old Testament, Daniel said, *"...the people* [who] *know their God shall be strong, and do exploits"* (Daniel 11:32).

ALL THINGS?

The more I learn about God and what He desires to do for me, the more powerful and meaningful my prayer life becomes.

David writes, *"I will cry unto God most high; unto God that performeth all things for me"* (Psalm 57:2).

What was Jesus really saying when He declared, *"And all things, whatsoever ye shall ask in prayer, believing, ye shall receive"* (Matthew 21:22)?

Does "whatsoever" truly mean "whatsoever"?

I've heard some people argue, "Oh, He was just referring to spiritual matters, so you shouldn't pray for the physical."

However, when Jesus says "all things," He means it! Any time you pray for God to affect a person's life it is both spiritual *and* physical.

"WHERE IS GOD?"

My friend, the Almighty God tells me to pray

because He desires change. The world may doubt, but when you are born again and become a member of God's family, He gives you the weapons and a heavenly force you can use to produce heaven-blessed transformation.

People ask, "Where is God?"

The answer is simple. He resides in the life and spirit of a believer who prays.

John Wesley believed little is accomplished on earth without people praying—because without their petitions God will not get involved.

The Father acts in response to the cries of His people.

SOMEBODY WAS PRAYING!

During the days of the early church, King Herod decided to persecute some of the followers of Christ. He murdered James, John's brother, and saw how much it pleased the Jews. So, during Passover Week, he arrested Peter and had him thrown into prison, intending for a public lynching after Passover.

However, the Bible records, *"...prayer was made without ceasing of the church unto God for him"* (Acts 12:1-5).

The Lord obviously heard them, because while Peter was sleeping—shackled to two soldiers— something amazing occurred: *"...behold, the angel of the Lord came upon him, and a light shined in the prison: and he smote Peter on the side, and raised him up, saying, Arise up quickly. And his chains fell off from his hands"* (v.7).

The angel told Peter to get dressed, to put on his shoes and follow him—which he did. The prison gate opened of its own accord and he was freed!

At first, Peter thought he was dreaming, but when he came to himself, he said, *"Now I know of a surety, that the Lord hath sent his angel, and hath delivered me out of the hand of Herod, and from all the expectation of the people of the Jews"* (v.11).

DYNAMIC POWER AND FAVOR

Reading this account leads me to ask the question: What would have happened to Peter if the believers had not prayed? I am convinced he would have remained imprisoned and faced death.

The prayers of the faithful moved the hand of God.

Peter quickly ran to the house of Mary, the mother of John, *"...where many were gathered together praying"* (v.12).

These believers didn't protest, petition the king or sign a letter begging for Peter's release. They prayed!

I believe there is a place in prayer where you have such access to God, such dynamic power and favor, that He will do *anything* for you. But this kind of praying always corresponds with powerful believing.

When a righteous child of God calls in Jesus' name, the devil is terrified because He knows change is on the horizon.

A troubled marriage is about to be healed. A rebellious teen is about to be delivered from drugs. A tortured soul is about to be set free!

God is waiting to move on your behalf and cause a miraculous transformation.

WHO WAS FOOLISH?

During the days of Hezekiah, the king of Assyria, Sennacherib, was capturing the cities of Judah and set his sights on Jerusalem. But Hezekiah rallied the people, encouraging them, *"Be strong and courageous, be not afraid nor dismayed for the king of Assyria, nor for all the multitude that is with him: for there be more with us than with him: with him is an arm of flesh; but with us is the Lord our God to help us, and to fight our battles"* (2 Chroniclse 32:7-8).

Yet, Sennacherib continued giving the people of Jerusalem a hard time, sending them message after message regarding how foolish they were to believe in only one God. Scripture details, *"He wrote also letters to rail on the Lord God of Israel, and to speak against him, saying, As the gods of the nations of other lands have not delivered their people out of mine hand, so shall not the God of Hezekiah deliver his people out of mine hand"* (v.17).

What an insulting statement!

CRYING UNTO HEAVEN

The volatile situation grew even worse when the invaders stood outside the walls of Jerusalem, shouting warnings that they were about to storm the city—attempting to demoralize the inhabitants.

What was King Hezekiah's response? Did he call a

conference to decide a plan of action? No, the Bible tells us how he and the prophet Isaiah, *"prayed and cried to heaven"* (v.20).

God not only heard their plea, He *"sent an angel, which cut off all the mighty men of valour, and the leaders and captains in the camp of the king of Assyria. So he returned with shame of face to his own land. And when he was come into the house of his god, they that came forth of his own bowels slew him there with the sword"* (v.21).

Prayer saved Hezekiah and the inhabitants of Jerusalem.

———————— ❦ ————————

The angel responded because he was listening to God, who in turn was listening to praying believers.

Remember, the Almighty says if His people who are called by His name will humble themselves, pray, seek His face and turn from their wicked ways, He promises to *"forgive their sin and will heal their land"* (2 Chronicles 7:14).

PRAYER CHANGES EVERYTHING!

Regardless of your present circumstances, the situation can be marvelously turned around:

- You can go from sickness to health through prayer.
- You can go from poverty to wealth through prayer.
- You can go from depression to deliverance through prayer.

The regrets of your past can be changed into hopes for the future and your broken heart can become one of strength and comfort. Believing prayer changes *everything!*

Chapter 8

The Prayer of Agreement

I remember the day I received a phone call from a grandmother in Oregon with what seemed like a very unusual prayer request. I knew the woman well, since she and her husband had been members of our Bible study before they moved to another city in our state.

On the phone, she asked, "Pastor André, I want you to pray and agree with me for the sun to start shining."

This peaked my curiosity. "Tell me what is happening," I asked.

She explained how she was in Oregon visiting her daughter and granddaughter. It was during the time of year when it rained a great deal in that part of the country—and it had been pouring for weeks.

So she called her husband at home and asked, "Honey, could you and the church agree with me that it would stop raining so I can spend some time at the beach with my granddaughter?"

Well, a few days went by with no sunshine, and, frustrated, she called home inquiring, "Are you sure you're praying? Because it is still raining."

After reaching me by phone she explained that she told her husband, "You are taking this far too casually. I am going to call Pastor André"—and she did.

"Would you pray with me for a sunny day? I want to spend at least one afternoon at the beach with my granddaughter before I come home."

My first reaction was, "Well, let's find a chapter and verse for this. We need to see what the Word says."

ROLLING BACK THE CLOUDS

I opened the Bible to the book of James 5 where it tells how Elijah *"prayed earnestly that it might not rain: and it rained not on the earth by the space of three years and six months"* (James 5:17).

Actually there are several examples in the Bible referring to God impacting the weather (Leviticus 26:3,4; Revelation16:8,9,21).

I agreed with this dear woman in Jesus' name, and before I hung up the phone, she exclaimed, "Pastor, the clouds are rolling back!"

A few days later I received a wonderful letter from her telling how she and her granddaughter got into the car while it was still drizzling, and headed to the beach. They spent four wonderful hours enjoying sunny skies. She wrote, "People in the area were surprised at the sudden change of weather, but we knew what really happened. It was our agreement in prayer."

The woman also noted that just as she left the beach the downpour resumed, and it continued until her return to North Carolina.

You may wonder, "Why would God even bother with such a trivial request?"

Regarding His children, nothing
is too small when we unite in prayer.

"It Shall Be Done"

Agreement is a potent spiritual weapon—and we need to utilize it just as we exercise prayer, worship, faith, giving and believing.

Jesus says, *"Whatsoever ye shall bind on earth shall be bound in heaven: and whatsoever ye shall loose on earth shall be loosed in heaven. Again I say unto you, That if two of you shall agree on earth as touching any thing that they shall ask, it shall be done for them of my Father which is in heaven. For where two or three are gathered together in my name, there am I in the midst of them"* (Matthew 18:20).

111

Certainly the Lord has the capacity to do whatever He desires, yet He asks us to be in like mind with Him here on earth.

*When our hearts are beating as one
in faith, miracles multiply!*

SPEAK "THE SAME THING"

Many seem to think the crisis they are going through at the moment is the worst disaster that could ever happen to them—the alpha and omega of their existence. However, there is something far greater than your current circumstance; it's called God's Word. When you exercise faith, the Word, the Holy Spirit and angels move on behalf of your situation. And, according to Scripture, the power of agreement is one of the primary ways the Lord operates.

In the words of the apostle Paul, *"I beseech you, brethren...that ye all speak the same thing, and that there be no divisions among you; but that ye be perfectly joined together in the same mind and in the same judgment"* (1 Corinthians 1:10).

CLAIMING THE PROMISES

A business friend of mine was half a million dollars in debt and his future seemed grim. I could visibly see how the stress was affecting every aspect of his life.

One day while I was praying, God impressed on my spirit that I could help this person. In the natural it seemed impossible. I certainly didn't have the finances to bail him out, but the Lord had another plan in mind.

I thanked God for the affirmation that I was to enter into a covenant of agreement with my friend regarding this matter. So I met with him and said, "Let's agree to see this mountain of debt disappear" —and I shared Scriptures declaring God's intent for His children to prosper.

Every time we got together, we claimed the divine promises and were in one accord regarding his business.

In less than two years the red ink had completely been erased. His client base expanded and exciting new contracts were being signed. The debt was gone and the value of his company increased enormously.

There is no doubt in my mind that God worked supernaturally in this situation because He saw the sincerity and strength of our spiritual alliance.

THE DANGER OF DIVISION

Dissension and disagreement will ruin your best efforts. It gives Satan the opening he is looking for to destroy marriages, businesses, churches, homes and lives. Jesus speaks to this issue when He says, *"Every kingdom divided against itself is brought to desolation; and every city or house divided against itself shall not stand"* (Matthew 12:25).

But when a covenant of harmony prevails, God recognizes the fact and releases His resources so He will receive the glory.

AN UNHOLY ALLIANCE

The perils of walking in discord and strife can be disastrous.

In the early church, the believers were so committed to spreading the Gospel, they actually sold their lands and earthly possessions so the message of Christ could go forward. However, Scripture records how a man named Ananias, with Sapphira his wife, sold a property and kept back a certain part of the proceeds before laying the rest at the apostles' feet (Acts 5:2).

But Peter said, *"Ananias, why hath Satan filled thine heart to lie to the Holy Ghost, and to keep back part of the price of the land?"* (v.3).

The apostle wanted to know what caused him to pull a trick like this. "You didn't lie to man," Peter told him, "but to God."

When Ananias heard these words, he *"fell down, and gave up the ghost: and great fear came on all them that heard these things. And the young men arose...carried him out, and buried him"* (vv.5-6).

About three hours later, Sapphira, not knowing what had happened, returned, and Peter asked her, *"Tell me whether ye sold the land for so much? And she said, Yea, for so much. Then Peter said unto her, How is it that ye have agreed together to tempt the Spirit of the Lord? behold, the feet of them which have buried thy husband are at the door, and shall carry thee out"* (vv.8-9).

At that very moment Sapphira died. *"Then fell she down straightway at his feet, and yielded up the ghost: and the young men came in, and found her dead, and, carrying her forth, buried her by her husband"* (v.10).

The deceptive agreement of Ananais and Sapphira to lie to the Holy Ghost brought their total destruction.

Never enter into a treaty with Satan.
He was a liar from the beginning and is
still deceiving people today.

A PACT WITH THE WORLD?

Paul, writing to the believers in Corinth, gives a warning on the dangers of forming bonds with the world. *"Be ye not unequally yoked together with unbelievers: for what fellowship hath righteousness with unrighteousness? and what communion hath*

*light with darkness? And what concord hath Christ
with Belial? or what part hath he that believeth with
an infidel? And what agreement hath the temple of
God with idols? for ye are the temple of the living
God; as God hath said, I will dwell in them, and walk
in them; and I will be their God, and they shall be my
people"* (2 Corinthians 6:14-16).

The apostle teaches there is to be no agreement or
"concord" between those who believe and those who
don't. But as the temple of God on earth, the Lord says
He will dwell with you. So when we link our lives to
other Christians, the Lord blesses our combined
efforts.

"WE CAN TAKE IT!"

For forty years the children of Israel wandered in
the wilderness because of their whining, complaining
and discontent. Even when Moses sent the twelve
spies to check out the land of Canaan, ten returned
with a negative report. They saw nothing but giants in
the land: *"We be not able to go up against the people;
for they are stronger than we"* (Numbers 13:31). This
pessimism spread like a virus among the Israelites,
until they were crying, *"Would God that we had died
in the land of Egypt!"* (Numbers 14:2).

Caleb and Joshua, however, had a totally different
perspective. They saw a land flowing with milk and

honey and said, "We can take it!"

Because they were in agreement with God, these two men and their families were the only ones to make it to the Promised Land.

IN HARMONY WITH HEAVEN

The prayer of agreement is an amazing way to see God move.

The prophet Isaiah asks, *"Who hath believed our report? and to whom is the arm of the Lord revealed?"* (Isaiah 53:1). It is made known to those who believe and are in harmony with the Father.

The problem we see may not be the real issue. Rather, our troubles persist because we don't accept what the Word declares. Agreement involves believing—and when you trust God, you are telling Him, "I agree with what You have said."

- Your Word declares you will deliver me in time of trouble (Psalm 34:19).
- Your Word says I can take the message of Christ to the nations (Mark 16:15).
- Your Word tells me I can minister to the sick (Mark 16:18).
- Your Word affirms that no weapon formed against me will prosper (Isaiah 54:17).
- Your Word promises You will shower me with blessings (Deuteronomy 28:2-6).

Never forget, *"the eyes of the Lord run to and fro throughout the whole earth, to show himself strong in the behalf of them whose heart is perfect toward him"* (2 Chronicles 16:9).

_____ ❦ _____

Your heart and His—this is perfect unity!

When you respond, "Yes, Lord," it tells the Father you are in covenant together, *"For all the promises of God in him are yea, and in him Amen, unto the glory of God by us"* (2 Corinthians 1:20).

NO DISTANCE IN PRAYER

Because of our worldwide ministry, I can confirm that prayers of agreement traverse time and space. For instance, I can be in one accord with a partner in Malaysia for a situation in Germany and God will intervene. This elimination of geographical barriers is possible because the Lord promises that if we agree on earth, the Father begins to move on our behalf (Matthew 18:19).

You do not even have to physically be in the same room. It's the divine agreement which involves God and brings victory.

Will you find an individual with whom you can

agree? It may not be a member of your family, but a prayer warrior in your church. Share the prayer of your heart and together bring the matter before the Lord.

Over the years I have found certain believers with whom I share what the Lord is telling me and where He is leading. I'm not looking for "yes men" to bolster a personal decision, rather those who will also seek God for His guidance regarding the matter. If we are both in one accord, we take it to the Father in prayer—and He responds.

I am encouraging you to form a spiritual alliance and to enter into a covenant with God. Together, experience the marvelous results which spring from the prayer of agreement.

CHAPTER 9

YOUR PARTNERSHIP WITH GOD

W hen faith is absent, the doors of heaven are locked.

In the Garden of Eden, when Adam and Eve rebelled against the Creator, there were two tragic results: (1) God was shut out from man and (2) man was shut out from God. It wasn't just that the first human beings were banished from the Garden, the Father became estranged from their lives.

To hide the shame of their nakedness, a lamb had to be slaughtered and blood spilled so they would have a covering. This was symbolic of what would take place thousands of years later at Calvary.

WE ARE PART OF HIS PLAN

After the fall of Adam, when God searched the earth to find a man with whom He could establish a covenant, He chose an individual called Abram —whose name He later changed to Abraham: "Father of many nations."

What qualities did the Almighty see in this individual which were different from those of his generation? Here was a man who would live by faith—with total reliance on God's leading. Scripture records, *"By faith Abraham, when he was called to go out into a place which he should after receive for an inheritance, obeyed; and he went out, not knowing whither he went"* (Hebrews 11:8).

Why did God need Abraham to live by faith? And why do we read he *"prayed unto God"*(Genesis 20:17)? Because without belief and prayer, the Lord will not move upon our situation.

God's plan includes our prayers to Him.

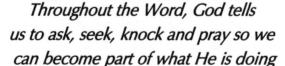

Throughout the Word, God tells us to ask, seek, knock and pray so we can become part of what He is doing on earth—to be His partners.

Before you were saved, the convicting power of the

Holy Spirit touched your life for one purpose—so you could pray. In fact, the very act of salvation begins with a heartfelt prayer—you say, "Jesus, please help me," and ask Christ to come into your heart so His blood can cleanse your sin.

By asking for divine assistance, you make contact with the Father.

REVERSE THE CURSE!

In Abraham's day, God told him, *"As for me, behold, my covenant is with thee, and thou shalt be a father of many nations"* (Genesis 17:4).

Remember, from Adam until this time, man was living under the curse, but through the Word of God spoken to Abraham, the Lord was revealing a better way. This is why I tell people today, "With chapter and verse, you reverse the curse!"

Without Scripture we don't realize the darkness we have been living in. As one new convert told me, "I was headed for hell and didn't know it. But when I heard God's Word, I realized, "That's me!" And I was set free!

Faith establishes the connection to the Almighty and His Kingdom. It is the door and entry point to our access and involvement with the Father.

Take a close look at your life. As a believer, you are not to be confused by carnality or lost to Satan. You are born again—a totally new creature in Christ Jesus.

Since this is true, start walking, talking, thinking and acting accordingly! *"For ye were sometimes darkness, but now are ye light in the Lord: walk as children of light"* (Ephesians 5:8).

I still meet those who question, "Am I truly saved?" "Is God really talking to me?" "Lord, are you sure You want me to do this?"

Yes! Your Heavenly Father is speaking to you!

TOO TIRED?

Praying "just a little" is the most frustrating thing you will ever do as a Christian. It is like being introduced to Almighty God, but having no meaningful conversation.

Our flesh says, "Don't worry. Just pray a few minutes and go on with your business."

The devil will whisper, "You need to quit praying. Your favorite TV show is about to start." Or, "It's time to eat. Why not take a break?"

How do you expect to solve a three hour problem with a quick three minute prayer? When there is a mountain that needs to be removed, don't linger in the foothills!

If you tell yourself it's time to pray, your body will likely respond, "I'm too tired!" But the same exhausted person who complains they can't fellowship with God will stay awake through an epic movie such as *Titanic*—which lasts well over three hours.

Who is in charge, you or your body? Take command and decide, "I'm getting up! It's time to pray!"

The Word tells us *"they that are in the flesh cannot please God. But ye are not in the flesh, but in the Spirit, if so be that the Spirit of God dwell in you. Now if any man have not the Spirit of Christ, he is none of his"* (Romans 8:8-9).

Allow God's Spirit to energize you!

PUTTING IT ALL TOGETHER

As followers of Christ, inside of us are many elements: the Holy Spirit, the light and life of God, dominion, authority and spiritual gifts. But how do we flow with these divine enablements to become an effective Christian?

125

How are we going to sort these factors out? It won't be by watching soap operas, football games or the news on CNN.

———— ❦ ————

It is through prayer we harness our belief and focus our faith.

As we continue to stay in fellowship with the Lord we begin to see where each element fits in and how it flows in the landscape of our spirituality.

Paul tells you to *"work out your own salvation with fear and trembling"* (Philippians 2:12). This is only possible through a partnership with the Father: *"For it is God which worketh in you both to will and to do of his good pleasure"* (v.13).

Let's face it, we don't have the mental capacity to figure out what only God can explain. As Paul writes, *"Now we have received, not the spirit of the world, but the spirit which is of God; that we might know the things that are freely given to us of God"* (1 Corinthians 2:12)

When God gave Abraham the promises, they didn't just happen with the Creator snapping His fingers. No, Abraham had to exercise his faith before the prophecy became a reality. Sure, the expectations were high, but he *"staggered not at the promise of God through unbelief; but was strong in faith, giving glory to God"* (Romans 4:20).

With the Lord's help, Abraham was able to "work out" what the Lord had placed in his heart, soul and mind.

DON'T SKIP THE BASICS

Some people balk at God's requirements. They don't want to "study to show themselves approved" or do what it takes to pass the Lord's inspection. Instead, they think it's possible to hop, skip and jump over the prerequisites and suggest, "Lord, just give me the signs, and wonders."

A few years ago, when I decided to learn to play the guitar, one of my teachers explained, "Well, here's what you need to do"—and he began telling me about chord formations, bars, music theory, etc.

"Hey, I just want to play," I impatiently told him. "I'll learn that stuff later."

But he was right. Without mastering the basics, we will never reach our objective.

ANDRÉ GORHAM

A POWERFUL PARTNERSHIP

In God's Kingdom, the *works* and manifestations come as a result of the Lord changing us on the inside—which is only possible through prayer.

In the book of Acts, the apostles weren't boastfully traveling through the land announcing, "I am a prophet. I have a Word from God for you." No, they were men of prayer—and their partnership with the Lord was the source of their power:

- On the day of Pentecost the 120 who gathered in the Upper Room were *"with one accord in prayer"* (Acts 1:14).
- The apostles gave themselves *"continually to prayer, and to the ministry of the word"* (Acts 6:4).
- In a gathering of believers, *"when they had prayed, the place was shaken where they were assembled together; and they were all filled with the Holy Ghost, and they spake the word of God with boldness"* (Acts 4:31).
- Peter was called to the city of Joppa because a woman named Tabitha had died. The Bible records how he *"kneeled down, and prayed; and turning him to the body said, Tabitha,*

128

arise. And she opened her eyes: and when she saw Peter, she sat up" (Acts 9:40).

WORKING TOGETHER

Because of prayer, we are able to be involved in an eternal partnership—and become laborers together with Him (1 Corinthians 3:9).

At salvation a spiritual merger takes place. From that moment forward, as a child and an heir, all that belongs to Him is yours, and all that belong to you is His (John 17:10).

The benefits are far too numerous to mention since He provides both the resources and the rewards.

Through the awesome power of prayer we work together to defeat Satan and help bring the message of redemption to the world.

Praise God, we have been chosen to experience this glorious privilege!

10 CHECKPOINTS
TO DETERMINE IF YOU WILL RECEIVE WHAT YOU SAY YOU BELIEVE

The principles of prayer found in this book will wither and die unless they are planted into your life and nourished daily.

To assess and examine where you stand with God regarding your prayer life, please give your honest answers to these 10 Checkpoints. They will help you identify your areas of weakness and the Scripture references will guide your spiritual growth:

1. Do I truly understand how and why prayer works?

■ What is the relationship between God's love and prayer (Psalm 91:14-15; John 3:16; 1 John 3:1-2)?

- How does the work of Christ at Calvary affect prayer (Luke 22:20; Hebrews 4:16; 10:16-17)?
- What is the result of being "God's elect" (2 Corinthians 5:17; James 5:13-15; Colossians 3:11; 1 Peter 2:5,9-10)?
- How does being the righteous of God in Jesus Christ impact answered prayers (2 Corinthians 5:21-22; 1 Peter 3:12,16)?
- What does His Word and His will have to do with prayers being answered (John 15:7; James 1:22-25; 1 John 5:14-15)?
- Why do we need to be specific when we pray (Mark 11:23-24; Mark 10:47-51)?

2. Is my prayer effective?

- What is the result of "effectual fervent prayer (James 5:16)?
- What does the Bible say about "believing" in relation to prayer (Matthew 9:28; 21:22; Hebrew 11:6)?
- Why should your prayers be backed up by Scripture (1 John 1:7; Psalm 119:11)?
- How does casting our cares on the Lord relate to praying (Mark 4:19; 1 Peter 5:6-7)?

- Why should we add thanksgiving to our prayers (John 11:41-43; 1 Thessalonians 5:18)?
- What does the Word say concerning how long we should pray (Acts 6:4; Luke 18:1; 1 Thessalonians 5:17)?

3. Are my prayers accompanied by power?

- What are the "weapons of our warfare" (2 Corinthians 10:4-5)?
- What was the result of the apostles praying for members of the early church (Acts 6:4-7)?
- How was the power of prayer evident in the lives of Abraham, Moses and Elisha (Genesis 20:17. Numbers 11:2; 2 Kings 6:17)?
- Why did Jesus pray (Luke 6:12-13)?
- What was the result of Daniel's powerful prayer (Daniel 2)?

4. How can I know God is listening ?

- What does it mean to ask "amiss" (James 4:1-2)?

- Does the Lord hear our thoughts (Ephesians 3:20)?
- Does God make promises to His children on earth (Romans 4:17-22; 2 Peter 3:9)?
- Specifically, what does the Bible say concerning God hearing our prayers (Psalm 4:3; 6:9; 34:4; 116:1-2; 1 Peter 3:12; 1 John 3:22)?

5. What characteristics do I need to possess to be successful in prayer?

- Why is an intimate knowledge of God's Word and His will necessary (John 15:7; 1 John 2:17; 5:14)?
- Are you diligent in your prayer life (Hebrews 11:6; 1 Peter 1:5-8 Proverbs 4:23)?
- Do you pray with determination (Luke 18:1-8)?
- Do you pray aggressively (Genesis 32:26-30; Matthew 11:12; 16:23; 2 Corinthians 10:4)?
- Are you patient with the Lord (Romans 15:4; Hebrews 6:14-15; 10:35-37; James1:3-4)?
- Do you trust God instead of man (Psalm 20:7; 1 Timothy 6:17)?

6. What is the source of true prayer?

- Do I have a precise desire (Mark 11:24)?
- Do I have a strong belief God will help me (2 Chronicles 20:3-12; Psalm 46:1; 121:1; Hebrews 4:16)?
- Do I understand the answer is beyond my own capabilities (2 Corinthians 12:9-10)?
- Is my request truly directed toward God rather than the situation (Ephesians 3:14,20; Psalm 2:8; 2 Chronicles 32:18-20)?

7. What preparations should I make for prayer?

- Why is it important to examine myself for fear, unbelief and unforgiveness (Psalm 66:17-20; Ezra 7:10, Mark 11:25-26)?
- What is the connection between the condition of my heart and answered prayer (1 John 3:19-22)?
- Am I developing my spiritual life through the knowledge of God's Word (Hosea 4:6; Luke 14:28-33)?

- Do I understand what it means to dwell in the "secret place" (Psalm 91:1; Matthew 6:6)?

8. How can I change a situation through prayer?

- Will the Lord respond to my faith (Mark 16:17)?
- Are their limits to God's ability to change things (Psalm 57:2; Genesis 18:14; Luke 1:37)?
- How does the Lord fight our battles (2 Chronicles 32:7-21)?

9. What is the prayer of agreement?

- Why does God ask us to join forces with other believers in prayer (Matthew 18:20)?
- Why is it vital that there be no division among us (Matthew 12:25; Acts 5: 1-10; 1 Corinthians 1:10)?
- What was the reward for the agreement of Joshua and Caleb (Numbers 14:24)?
- Will God send His angels to assist me (Hebrews 1:14; Psalm 103:20, Revelation 8:5)?

10. How can I form a prayer partnership with God?

- Am I assured the Lord will work on my behalf (Ephesians 5:8; Romans 8:8-9)?
- Will God help me solve earthly problems (1 Corinthians 2:12; Philippians 2:12-13)?
- As a believer, is everything that belongs to God truly mine (John 17:10)?

A PERSONAL PRAYER AND BIBLE READING PLAN

Here is a simple but effective strategy the Lord gave me to provide consistency and balance to those who desire to strengthen their prayer and study of Scripture.

I am asking you to commit to this program for 31 minutes each day.

Pray 8 minutes in your spirit man (Jude 1:20). Meditation, thoughtfulness and spiritual reflection (Ephesians 3:20,).

Pray 8 minutes in the natural (Acts 6:4).
Specifically pray for:
Leaders and those in authority: The President and Vice President, members of Congress, state and local governmental officials (1 Timothy 2:1-4).

Your family: Spouse, children, mother, father, sisters, brothers, extended family members, friends—and yourself.

Your finances: Tithes, offerings, employment, mortgage/rent, monthly payments, entertainment, clothing and food, gifts and loans to others.

Your future: The Father's plan for your life in any specific area (Jeremiah 29:11).

Read God's Word for 15 minutes.
(2 Timothy 2:15; 2 Timothy 3:14-17).

January – 1 John
February – Acts
March – Romans
April – 1 and 2 Corinthians
May – Galatians and Ephesians
June – Philippians and Colossians
July – 1 and 2 Thessalonians
August – 1 and 2 Timothy
September – Titus and Philemon
October – Hebrews and James
November – 1and 2 Peter
December – 2 and 3 John, Jude and Revelation

It is likely you will finish your reading assignment early in the month. If so, go back to the beginning and study the verses carefully again.

You are *"Always in every prayer of mine making request with joy"* (Philippians 1:4). I am remembering you *"fervently...in prayers, that ye may stand perfect and complete in all the will of God"* (Colossians 4:12).

May the Lord give you joy unspeakable—filled with His glory.

– André Gorham

For a Complete List of Resources, or to
Schedule the Author for Speaking
Engagements, Contact:

André Gorham
Anointed Word Ministries
Phone: 919-598-1879
Internet: www.anointed.org
Email: pastor@anointed.org

Community Fellowship International Church
1812 Riddle Road
Durham, NC 27713
Phone: 919-598-8555